My Sight Word List

a	in	aid
and	is	see
away	it	the
big	jump	three
blue	little	to
can	look	two
come	make	up
down	me	we
find	my	where
for	not	yellow
funny	one	you
go	day	
help	play	
here	red	
I	run	

Name: _______________ Date: _______________

Today is: Monday Tuesday Wednesday Thursday Friday

Direction: Trace and read the sentences.

amusement	pistolet	courir	soleil
godere	pistola	correre	sole

They are having fun.

He has a gun.

The bear is running.

The sun is smiling.

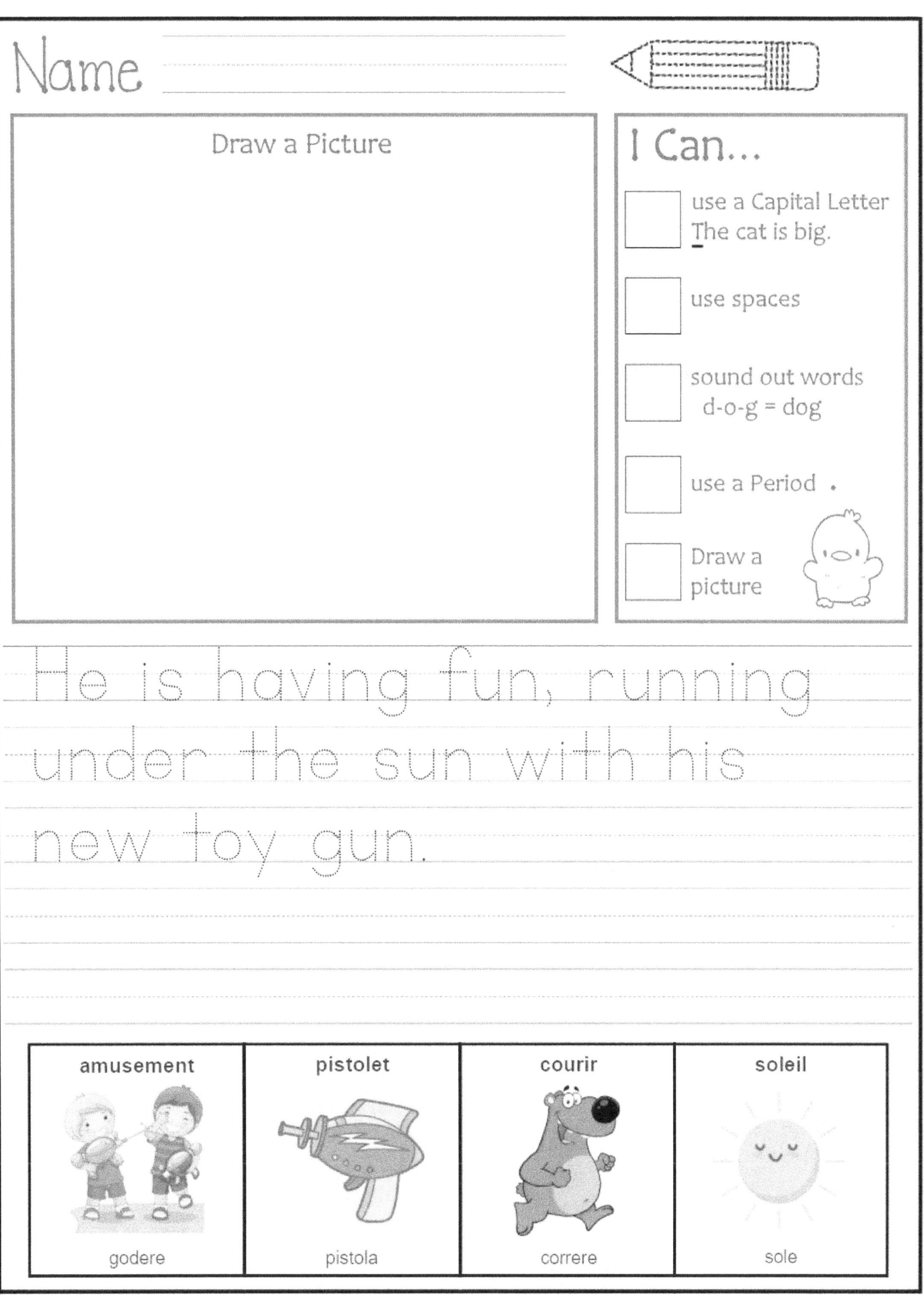

Name
Draw a Picture
I Can...
use a Capital Letter
The cat is big.
use spaces
sound out words
d-o-g = dog
use a Period .
Draw a
picture
He is having fun, running under the sun with his new toy gun.
amusement
godere
pistolet
pistola
courir
correre
soleil
sole

Name: ______________________ Date: ______________________

Today is: Monday Tuesday Wednesday Thursday Friday

Direction: Trace and read the sentences.

sac	chiffon	étiquette	remuer

sacchetto	straccio	etichetta	scodinzolante

He has many bags.

I see a rag.

I see a tag.

Its tail is wagging.

Draw a Picture

I Can...

- [ ] use a Capital Letter
  The cat is big.
- [ ] use spaces
- [ ] sound out words
  d-o-g = dog
- [ ] use a Period .
- [ ] Draw a picture

The bag on the rag has
a blue tag which made
the dog's tail wag.

sac	chiffon	étiquette	remuer
sacchetto	straccio	etichetta	scodinzolante

Name: ____________________ Date: ____________________

Today is: Monday Tuesday Wednesday Thursday Friday

Direction: Trace and read the sentences.

canettes	**homme**	**la poêle**	**van**
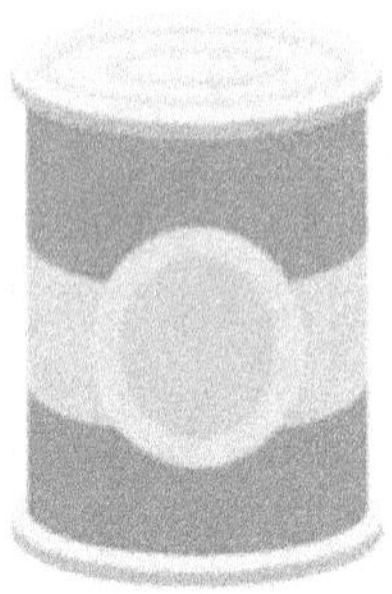			
lattine	uomo	padella	furgone

I see a can of soda.

The man is happy.

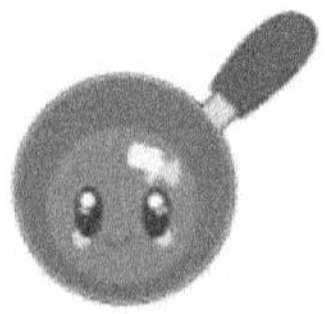

The pan is dirty.

I see a big van.

Draw a Picture

I Can...

- [ ] use a Capital Letter
  <u>T</u>he cat is big.

- [ ] use spaces

- [ ] sound out words
  d-o-g = dog

- [ ] use a Period .

- [ ] Draw a
  picture

The man who was driving
a van ran over a can
and a pan.

canettes	homme	la poêle	van
lattine	uomo	padella	furgone

Name: _________________________ Date: _________________

Today is: Monday   Tuesday   Wednesday
           Thursday   Friday

Direction: Trace and read the sentences.

couper	intestin	cabane	écrou
taglio	intestino	capanna	noce

He cut his nails.

He has a gut.

This is a small hut.

It is holding a nut.

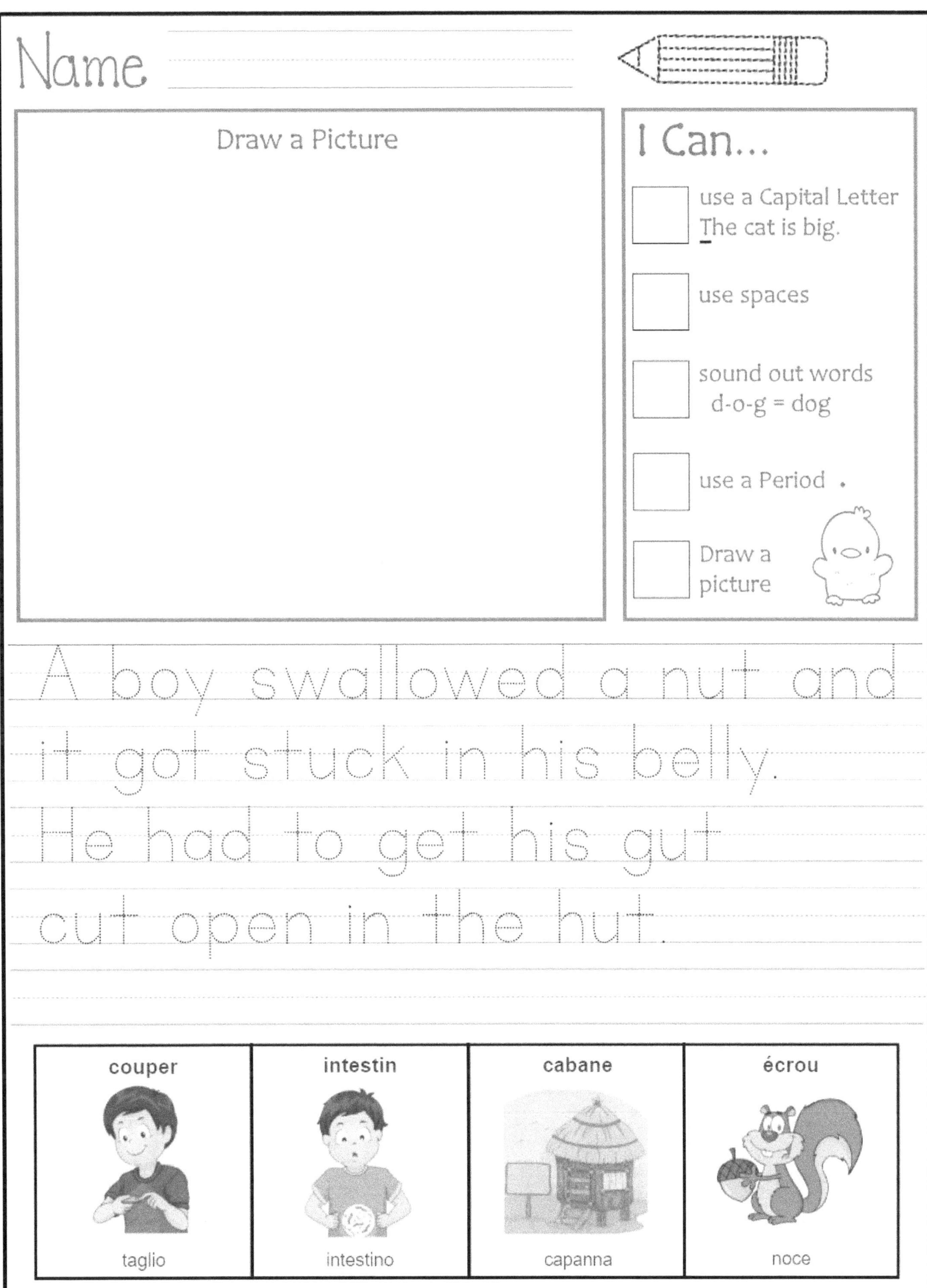

Name

Draw a Picture

I Can...

use a Capital Letter
The cat is big.

use spaces

sound out words
d-o-g = dog

use a Period .

Draw a
picture

A boy swallowed a nut and
it got stuck in his belly.
He had to get his gut
cut open in the hut.

couper
taglio

intestin
intestino

cabane
capanna

écrou
noce

Name: ____________________ Date: ____________________

Today is: Monday | Tuesday | Wednesday | Thursday | Friday

Direction: Trace and read the sentences.

graisse	chat	chapeau	tapis
		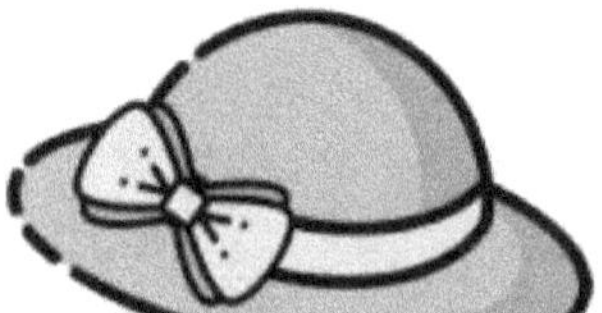	
grasso	gatto	cappello	stuoia

I see a fat dog.

This is my little cat.

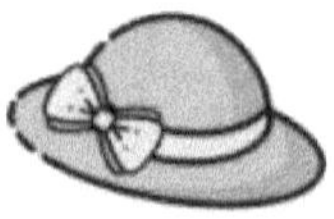

I like this hat.

I see a big mat.

Name

Draw a Picture

I Can...

- [ ] use a Capital Letter
  <u>T</u>he cat is big.

- [ ] use spaces

- [ ] sound out words
  d-o-g = dog

- [ ] use a Period .

- [ ] Draw a picture

The fat cat laid on the mat that was a hat pattern.

graisse	chat	chapeau	tapis
grasso	gatto	cappello	stuoia

Name: ____________________ Date: ____________________

Today is: Monday Tuesday Wednesday Thursday Friday

Direction: Trace and read the sentences.

taxi	laboratoire	languette	crabe

taxi	laboratorio	linguetta	granchio

The cab is fast.

The lab is exciting.

The tab is long.

We found a crab.

Draw a Picture

I Can...

- [ ] use a Capital Letter
  The cat is big.
- [ ] use spaces
- [ ] sound out words
  d-o-g = dog
- [ ] use a Period .
- [ ] Draw a picture

The crab called a cab to drive him to the lab and when he got off he paid his tab.

taxi	laboratoire	languette	crabe
TAXI			
taxi	laboratorio	linguetta	granchio

Name: ____________________ Date: ____________________

Today is: Monday Tuesday Wednesday Thursday Friday

Direction: Trace and read the sentences.

jambon	confiture	mouton	palourde
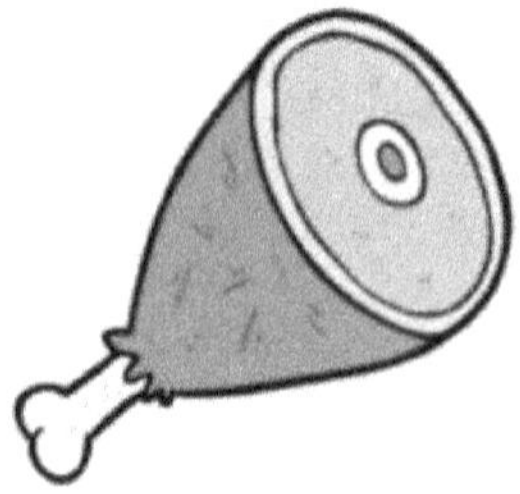	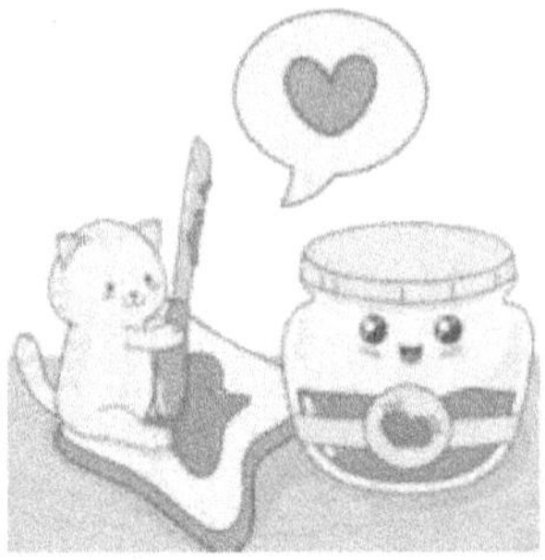	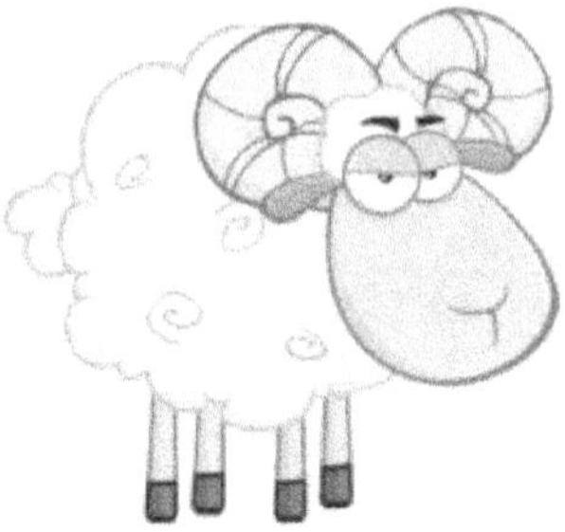	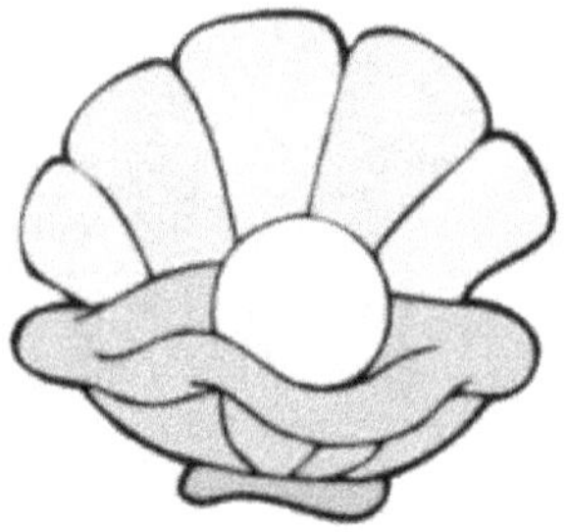
prosciutto	marmellata	pecora	mollusco

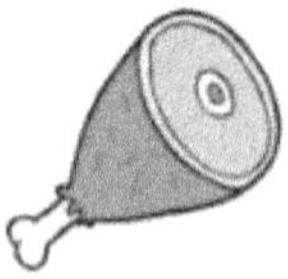 I like to eat ham.

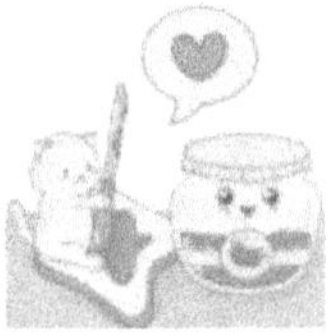 We like to eat jam.

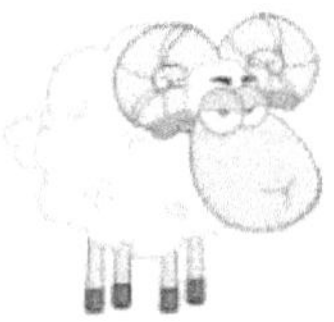 The ram is big.

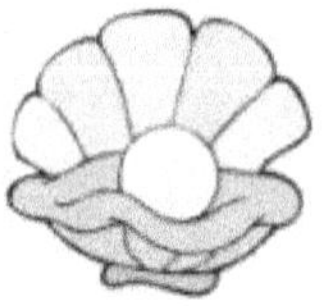 The clam is pretty.

Draw a Picture

I Can...

- [ ] use a Capital Letter
  <u>T</u>he cat is big.

- [ ] use spaces

- [ ] sound out words
  d-o-g = dog

- [ ] use a Period .

- [ ] Draw a picture

The clam gave the ram ham. Then the ram gave the clam jam.

jambon	confiture	mouton	palourde
prosciutto	marmellata	pecora	mollusco

Name: ____________________ Date: ____________________

Today is: Monday Tuesday Wednesday Thursday Friday

Direction: Trace and read the sentences.

lit	de premier plan	rouge	mariage
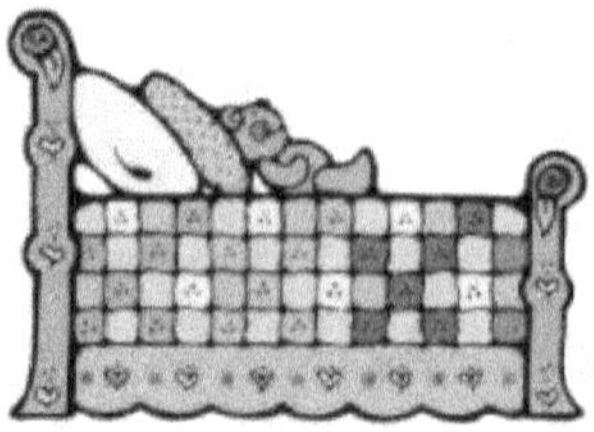			
letto	principale	rosso	nozze

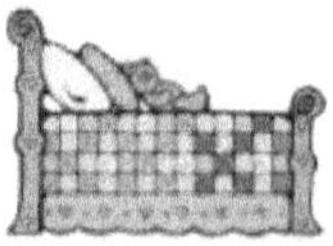 This is my little bed.

 He led us to safety.

 The apple is red.

 He asks her to wed.

Draw a Picture

I Can...

- [ ] use a Capital Letter
  The cat is big.
- [ ] use spaces
- [ ] sound out words
  d-o-g = dog
- [ ] use a Period .
- [ ] Draw a picture

When the prince got out of bed, he was led on a red carpet to be wed with the princess.

lit	de premier plan	rouge	mariage
letto	principale	rosso	nozze

Name: _______________ Date: _______________

Today is: Monday   Tuesday   Wednesday

Thursday   Friday

Direction: Trace and read the sentences.

mauvais	papa	furieux	triste
cattivo	papà	pazzo	triste

This apple is bad.

My dad is very kind.

The reindeer is mad.

The little cat is sad.

Draw a Picture

I Can...

- [ ] use a Capital Letter
  The cat is big.
- [ ] use spaces
- [ ] sound out words
  d-o-g = dog
- [ ] use a Period .
- [ ] Draw a picture

I was bad so my dad
got mad and now
I am so sad.

mauvais	papa	furieux	triste
cattivo	papà	pazzo	triste

Name: _______________ Date: _______________

Today is: [Monday] [Tuesday] [Wednesday]
[Thursday] [Friday]

Direction: Trace and read the sentences.

animal den	poule	écuries	dix
tana animale	gallina	stalle	dieci

It is a den.

The hens lay eggs.

She has a good pen.

The ten is smiling.

The hen that lived in the
pen laid ten eggs
in her den.

Name: ____________________ Date: ____________________

Today is: Monday | Tuesday | Wednesday | Thursday | Friday

Direction: Trace and read the sentences.

gommeux	maman	somme	tambour

gommoso	mamma	somma	tamburo

I like to chew gum.

My mum is kind!

I can do a sum!

The drum is big.

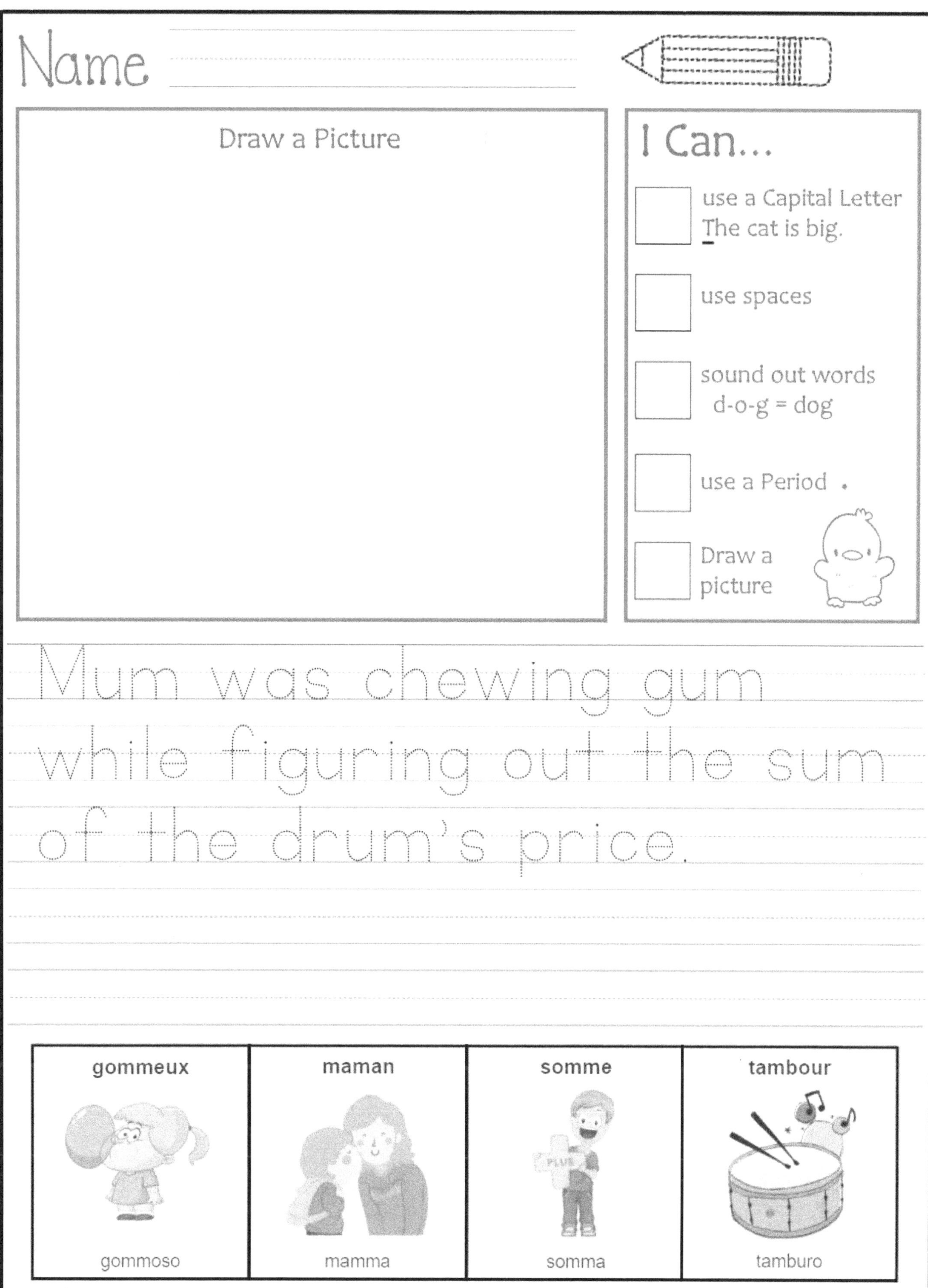

Name
Draw a Picture
I Can...
use a Capital Letter
The cat is big.
use spaces
sound out words
d-o-g = dog
use a Period .
Draw a picture
Mum was chewing gum while figuring out the sum of the drum's price.
gommeux
gommoso
maman
mamma
somme
somma
tambour
tamburo

Name: ____________________ Date: ____________________

Today is: Monday Tuesday Wednesday Thursday Friday

Direction: Trace and read the sentences.

offre	cacher	enfant	couvercle
			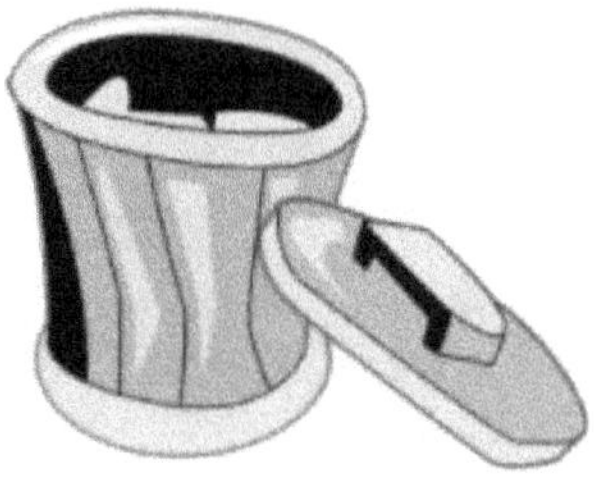
offerta	nascondere	ragazzo	coperchio

He likes to bid.

He is hiding.

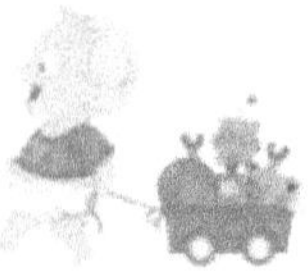

The kid like to play.

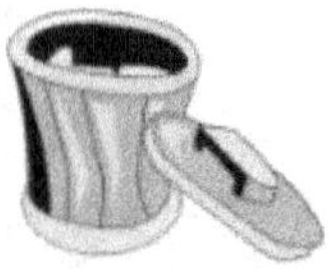

I see a lid.

Draw a Picture

I Can...

☐ use a Capital Letter
The cat is big.

☐ use spaces

☐ sound out words
d-o-g = dog

☐ use a Period .

☐ Draw a picture

The kid bid a lid for one hundred dollars then hid from his mad parents.

offre	cacher	enfant	couvercle
offerta	nascondere	ragazzo	coperchio

Name: ______________________ Date: ______________________

Today is: Monday Tuesday Wednesday Thursday Friday

Direction: Trace and read the sentences.

gros	creuser	porc	perruque

grande	scavare	maiale	parrucca

That is a big pencil.

He will dig up a hole.

The pig is fat.

She puts on a wig.

Draw a Picture

I Can...

- [ ] use a Capital Letter
  The cat is big.

- [ ] use spaces

- [ ] sound out words
  d-o-g = dog

- [ ] use a Period .

- [ ] Draw a picture

The big pig went to dig in the mud for his wig.

gros	creuser	porc	perruque
grande	scavare	maiale	parrucca

Name: ______________________ Date: ______________________

Today is: Monday Tuesday Wednesday Thursday Friday

Direction: Trace and read the sentences.

poubelle	ailette	épingle	gagner
	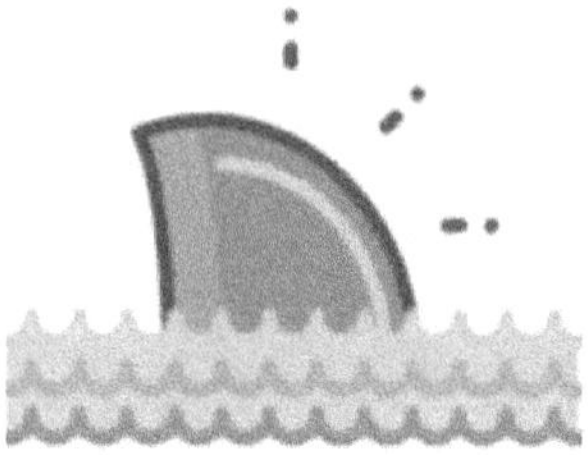		
bidone	pinna	perno	vincere

It is a recycle bin.

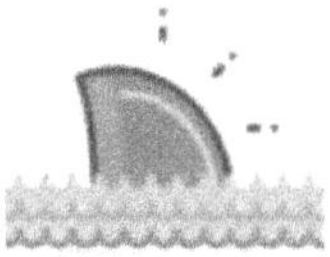
The shark has a fin.

The pin is pointy.

He won the match.

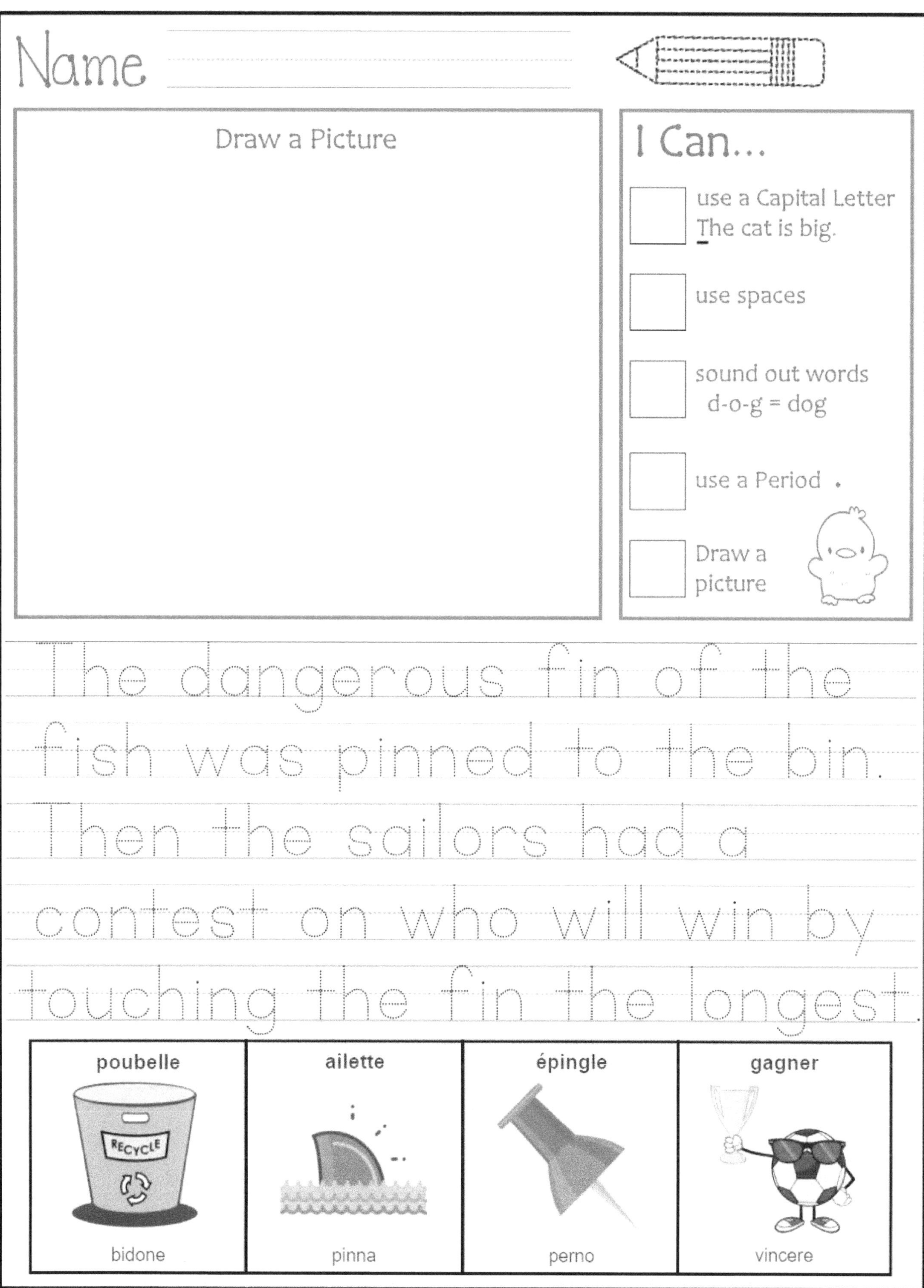
Name

Draw a Picture

I Can...

use a Capital Letter
The cat is big.

use spaces

sound out words
d-o-g = dog

use a Period .

Draw a
picture

The dangerous fin of the
fish was pinned to the bin.
Then the sailors had a
contest on who will win by
touching the fin the longest.

poubelle
RECYCLE
bidone

ailette
pinna

épingle
perno

gagner
vincere

Name: _________________ Date: ___________

Today is: Monday Tuesday Wednesday Thursday Friday

Direction: Trace and read the sentences.

hanche	lèvres	pincer	boisson
anca	labbra	pizzicare	bevanda

This is my hip.

Her lips are red.

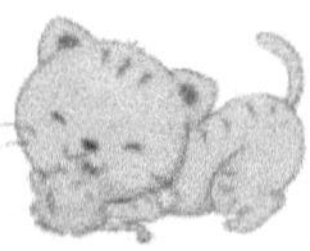

It is nipping its toy.

She is sipping.

The dog nipped someone who was sipping water with his lip.

hanche	lèvres	pincer	boisson
anca	labbra	pizzicare	bevanda

Name: ____________________ Date: ____________________

Today is: Monday Tuesday Wednesday Thursday Friday

Direction: Trace and read the sentences.

en forme	**frappé**	**trousse**	**asseoir**
		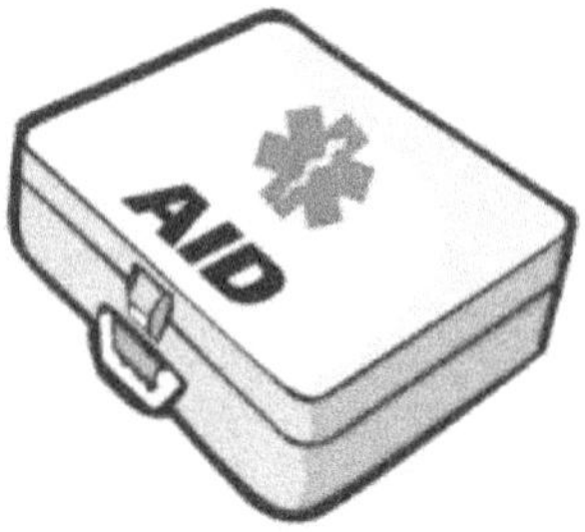 	
in forma	colpire	kit	sedersi

It is perfectly fit.

They hit each other.

That is a safety kit.

He is sitting.

Draw a Picture

I Can...

- [ ] use a Capital Letter
  The cat is big.

- [ ] use spaces

- [ ] sound out words
  d-o-g = dog

- [ ] use a Period .

- [ ] Draw a picture

The fit doctor sat then was hit by a kit.

en forme	frappé	trousse	asseoir
in forma	colpire	kit	sedersi

Name: ____________________ Date: ____________________

Today is: Monday Tuesday Wednesday Thursday Friday

Direction: Trace and read the sentences.

blé	emploi	rob	pleurer
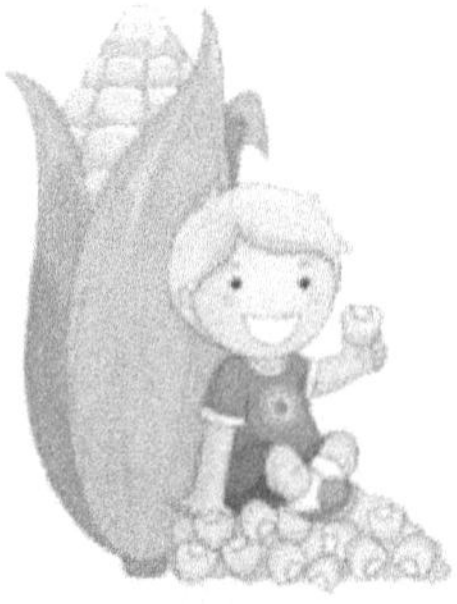	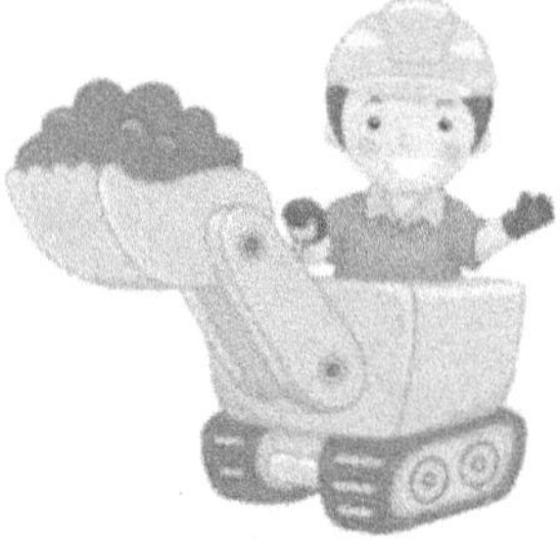	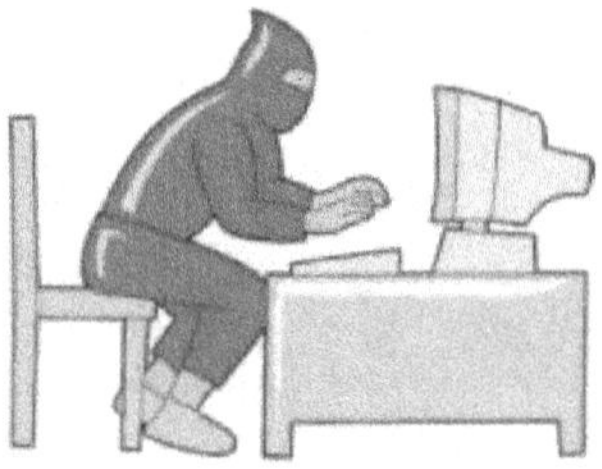	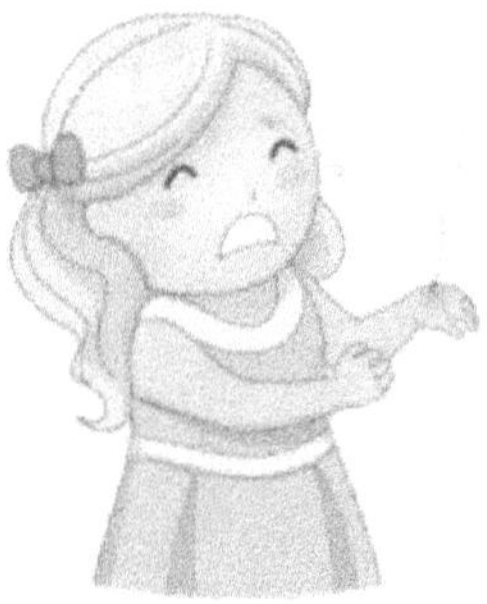
mais	lavoro	rapinare	piangere

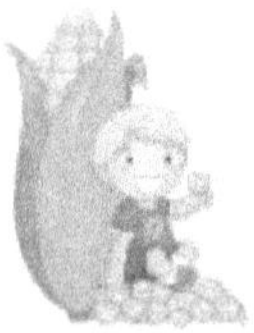

I ate corn on the cob.

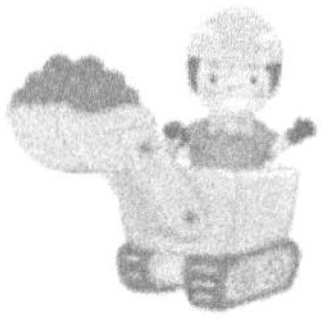

This is my job.

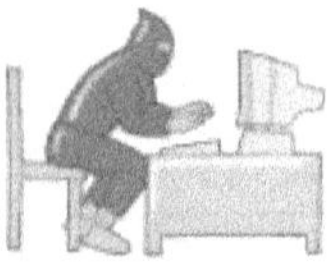

He is robbing.

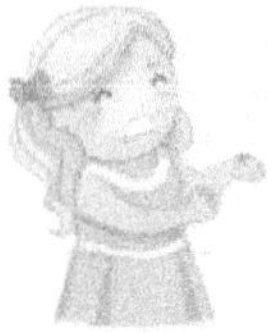

The girl is sobbing.

Draw a Picture

I Can...

- [ ] use a Capital Letter
  The cat is big.
- [ ] use spaces
- [ ] sound out words
  d-o-g = dog
- [ ] use a Period .
- [ ] Draw a picture

The chef robbed a corn cob and then was sobbing because he had lost his job.

blé	emploi	rob	pleurer
mais	lavoro	rapinare	piangere

Name: ______________________ Date: ______________________

Today is: Monday | Tuesday | Wednesday | Thursday | Friday

Direction: Trace and read the sentences.

chien	porc	le jogging	bois
			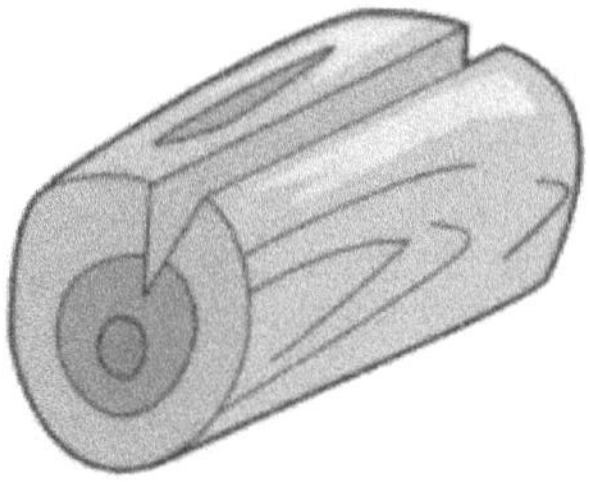
cane	maiale	jogging	legna

The dog is thrilled.

The hog is big.

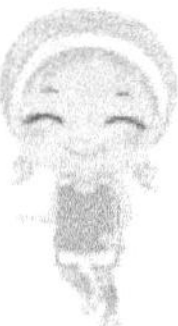

She is jogging.

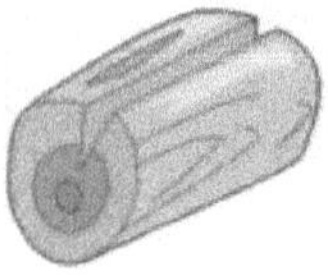

The log is small.

Name

Draw a Picture

I Can...

- [ ] use a Capital Letter
  <u>T</u>he cat is big.

- [ ] use spaces

- [ ] sound out words
  d-o-g = dog

- [ ] use a Period .

- [ ] Draw a picture

The dog and the hog went for a jog but then tripped on a log.

chien	porc	le jogging	bois
cane	maiale	jogging	legna

Name: _____________________ Date: _____________________

Today is: [Monday] [Tuesday] [Wednesday]
[Thursday] [Friday]

Direction: Trace and read the sentences.

punaise	étreinte	cruche	agresser
insetto	abbraccio	brocca	boccale

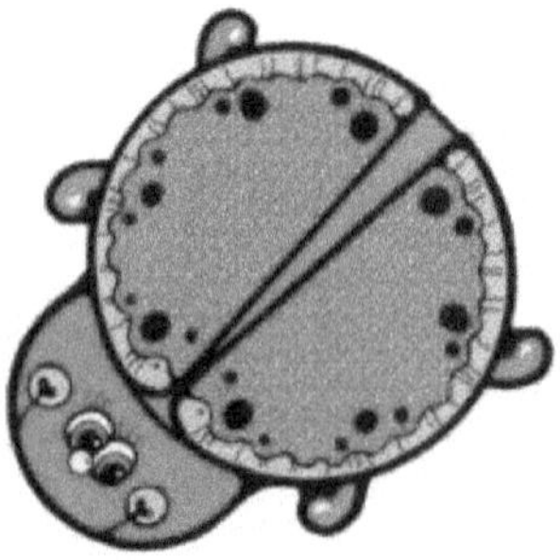

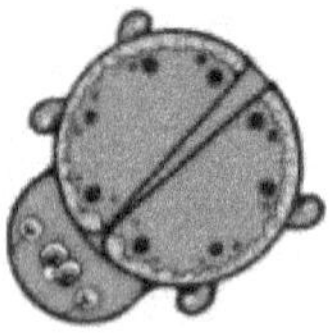

The bug is colorful.

She is hugging.

The jug has milk in it.

He has a mug.

Name

Draw a Picture

I Can...

☐ use a Capital Letter
  <u>T</u>he cat is big.

☐ use spaces

☐ sound out words
  d-o-g = dog

☐ use a Period .

☐ Draw a picture

The bug hugged the jug and the mug which was full of jam.

punaise	étreinte	cruche	agresser
insetto	abbraccio	brocca	boccale

Name: _______________ Date: _______________

Today is: Monday Tuesday Wednesday Thursday Friday

Direction: Trace and read the sentences.

lit	point	chaud	pot
letto	punto	caldo	pentola

This is my cot.

There are many dots.

It is very hot.

He has a plant pot.

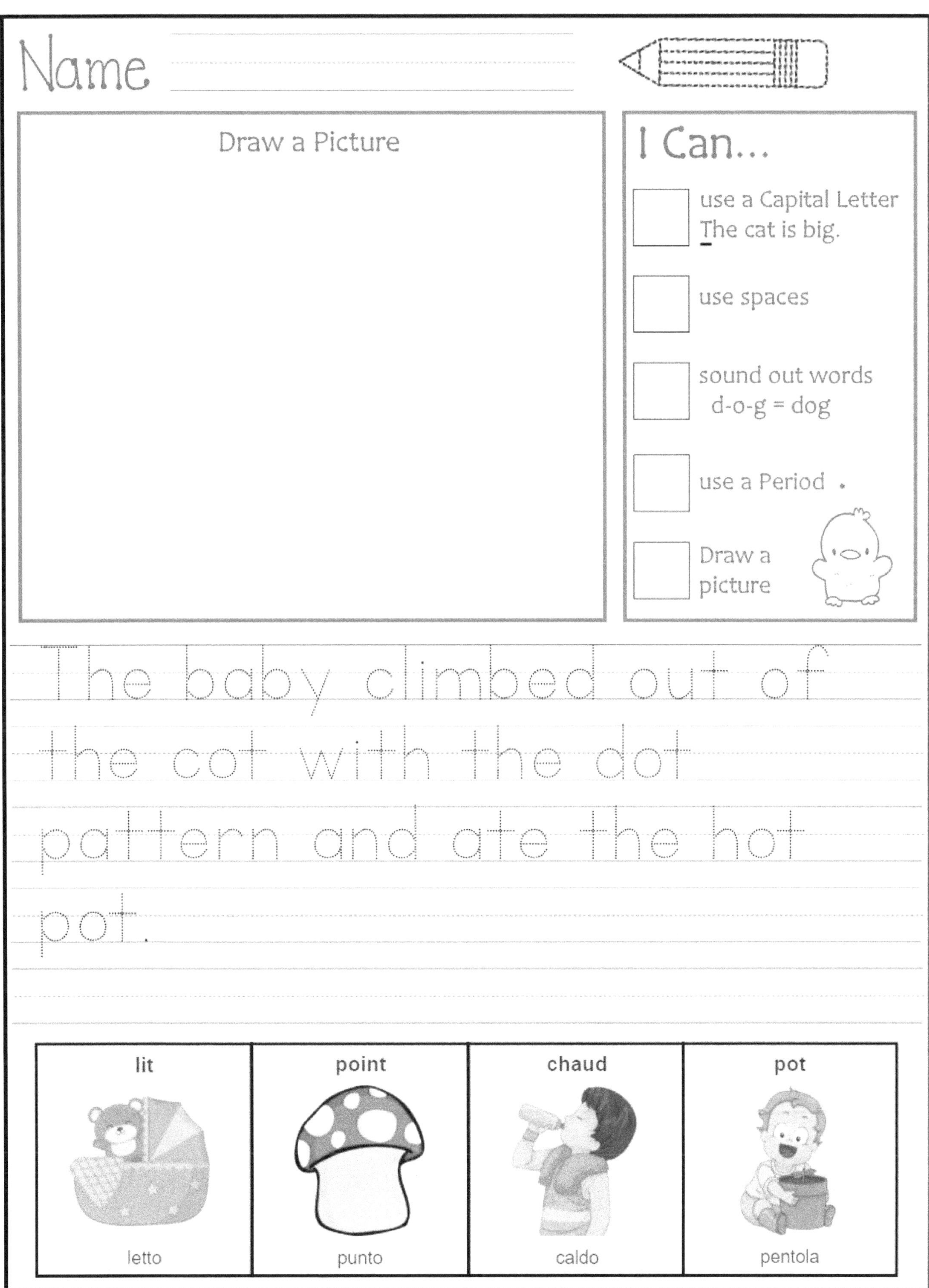

Name

Draw a Picture

I Can...

use a Capital Letter
The cat is big.

use spaces

sound out words
d-o-g = dog

use a Period .

Draw a
picture

The baby climbed out of the cot with the dot pattern and ate the hot pot.

lit
letto

point
punto

chaud
caldo

pot
pentola

Name: _________________________ Date: _________________________

Today is: Monday   Tuesday   Wednesday

Thursday   Friday

Direction: Read the words and make a sentence.

| amusement | pistolet | courir | soleil |
| godere | pistola | correre | sole |

____

____

____

____

Name

Draw a Picture

I Can...

- [ ] use a Capital Letter
  <u>T</u>he cat is big.

- [ ] use spaces

- [ ] sound out words
  d-o-g = dog

- [ ] use a Period .

- [ ] Draw a picture

Name: _________________ Date: _______

Today is: Monday Tuesday Wednesday
Thursday Friday

sac	chiffon	étiquette	remuer
sacchetto	straccio	etichetta	scodinzolante

Name

Draw a Picture

I Can...

- [ ] use a Capital Letter
  <u>T</u>he cat is big.

- [ ] use spaces

- [ ] sound out words
  d-o-g = dog

- [ ] use a Period .

- [ ] Draw a picture

Name: ___________________ Date: ___________

Today is: Monday Tuesday Wednesday Thursday Friday

Name: _________________________ Date: _______________

Today is: Monday | Tuesday | Wednesday
Thursday | Friday

Direction: Read the words and make a sentence.

canettes	homme	la poêle	van
lattine	uomo	padella	furgone

Name

Draw a Picture

I Can...

☐ use a Capital Letter
The cat is big.

☐ use spaces

☐ sound out words
d-o-g = dog

☐ use a Period .

☐ Draw a picture

Name: ___________________ Date: ___________________

Today is: Monday Tuesday Wednesday Thursday Friday

Name: _______________________ Date: _______________

Today is: Monday Tuesday Wednesday Thursday Friday

Direction: Read the words and make a sentence.

couper	intestin	cabane	écrou
taglio	intestino	capanna	noce

Draw a Picture

I Can...

☐ use a Capital Letter
The cat is big.

☐ use spaces

☐ sound out words
d-o-g = dog

☐ use a Period .

☐ Draw a picture

Name: _______________________   Date: _______________

Today is: [Monday] [Tuesday] [Wednesday]
          [Thursday] [Friday]

Name: _________________ Date: _________________

Today is: Monday   Tuesday   Wednesday

Thursday   Friday

Direction: Read the words and make a sentence.

graisse	chat	chapeau	tapis
grasso	gatto	cappello	stuoia

Name

Draw a Picture

I Can...

- ☐ use a Capital Letter
  The cat is big.

- ☐ use spaces

- ☐ sound out words
  d-o-g = dog

- ☐ use a Period .

- ☐ Draw a picture

Name: _______________________   Date: _______________

Today is: Monday | Tuesday | Wednesday | Thursday | Friday

Name: _______________________ Date: _______________

Today is: [Monday] [Tuesday] [Wednesday]
[Thursday] [Friday]

Direction: Read the words and make a sentence.

taxi	**laboratoire**	**languette**	**crabe**
taxi	laboratorio	linguetta	granchio

Name

Draw a Picture

I Can...

- [ ] use a Capital Letter
  <u>T</u>he cat is big.

- [ ] use spaces

- [ ] sound out words
  d-o-g = dog

- [ ] use a Period .

- [ ] Draw a picture

Name: _______________________   Date: _______________

Today is: | Monday | Tuesday | Wednesday |
          | Thursday | Friday |

jambon	confiture	mouton	palourde
prosciutto	marmellata	pecora	mollusco

Draw a Picture

I Can...

- ☐ use a Capital Letter
  The cat is big.

- ☐ use spaces

- ☐ sound out words
  d-o-g = dog

- ☐ use a Period .

- ☐ Draw a picture

Name: _________________ Date: _________

Today is: Monday Tuesday Wednesday Thursday Friday

Name: _________________________ Date: _________________

Today is: Monday Tuesday Wednesday Thursday Friday

Direction: Read the words and make a sentence.

lit	de premier plan	rouge	mariage
letto	principale	rosso	nozze

Name

Draw a Picture

I Can...

☐ use a Capital Letter
The cat is big.

☐ use spaces

☐ sound out words
d-o-g = dog

☐ use a Period .

☐ Draw a
picture

Name: _______________   Date: _______________

Today is:

| Monday | Tuesday | Wednesday |
| Thursday | Friday | |

Name: _________________ Date: _________________

Today is: | Monday | Tuesday | Wednesday |
| Thursday | Friday |

Direction: Read the words and make a sentence.

| mauvais | papa | furieux | triste |
| cattivo | papà | pazzo | triste |

Name

Draw a Picture

I Can...

- [ ] use a Capital Letter
  The cat is big.

- [ ] use spaces

- [ ] sound out words
  d-o-g = dog

- [ ] use a Period .

- [ ] Draw a
  picture

Name: _______________________ Date: _______________

Today is: Monday   Tuesday   Wednesday   Thursday   Friday

Name: ______________________ Date: ______________________

Today is: Monday Tuesday Wednesday Thursday Friday

Direction: Read the words and make a sentence.

animal den	poule	écuries	dix
			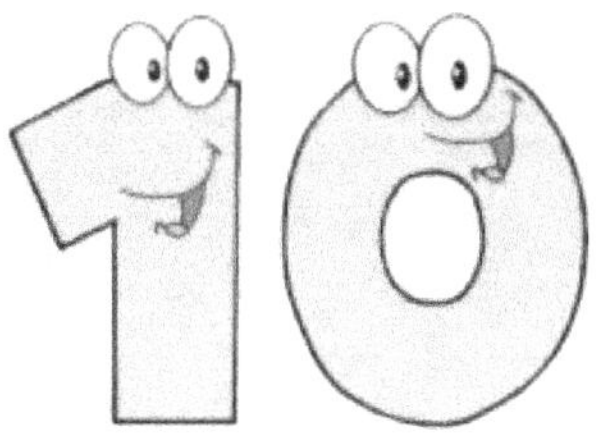
tana animale	gallina	stalle	dieci

____

____

____

____

Name

Draw a Picture

I Can...

- [ ] use a Capital Letter
  The cat is big.

- [ ] use spaces

- [ ] sound out words
  d-o-g = dog

- [ ] use a Period .

- [ ] Draw a picture

Name: _______________________ Date: _______________

Today is: Monday Tuesday Wednesday Thursday Friday

Name: ___________________ Date: ___________________

Today is: Monday   Tuesday   Wednesday

Thursday   Friday

Direction: Read the words and make a sentence.

gommeux	maman	somme	tambour
gommoso	mamma	somma	tamburo

Draw a Picture

I Can...

use a Capital Letter
The cat is big.

use spaces

sound out words
d-o-g = dog

use a Period .

Draw a
picture

Name: _______________________ Date: _______________________

Today is: Monday | Tuesday | Wednesday | Thursday | Friday

Name: _______________________ Date: _______________

Today is: Monday   Tuesday   Wednesday

Thursday   Friday

Direction: Read the words and make a sentence.

offre	**cacher**	**enfant**	**couvercle**
offerta	nascondere	ragazzo	coperchio

Name

Draw a Picture

I Can...

☐ use a Capital Letter
The cat is big.

☐ use spaces

☐ sound out words
d-o-g = dog

☐ use a Period .

☐ Draw a picture

Name: _______________________ Date: _______________

Today is: Monday Tuesday Wednesday Thursday Friday

Name: _______________ Date: _______________

Today is: [Monday] [Tuesday] [Wednesday]
[Thursday] [Friday]

Direction: Read the words and make a sentence.

gros	creuser	porc	perruque
grande	scavare	maiale	parrucca

Name _______________________________

Draw a Picture

I Can...

- [ ] use a Capital Letter
  The cat is big.

- [ ] use spaces

- [ ] sound out words
  d-o-g = dog

- [ ] use a Period .

- [ ] Draw a picture

Name: ___________________________ Date: ___________

Today is: Monday   Tuesday   Wednesday

Thursday   Friday

Name: _______________________ Date: _______________________

Today is: Monday Tuesday Wednesday Thursday Friday

Direction: Read the words and make a sentence.

poubelle	ailette	épingle	gagner
bidone	pinna	perno	vincere

Name

Draw a Picture

I Can...

- [ ] use a Capital Letter
  <u>T</u>he cat is big.

- [ ] use spaces

- [ ] sound out words
  d-o-g = dog

- [ ] use a Period .

- [ ] Draw a picture

Name: ___________________________ Date: ___________

Today is: Monday Tuesday Wednesday Thursday Friday

Name: _________________________ Date: _________________________

Today is: Monday | Tuesday | Wednesday
Thursday | Friday

Direction: Read the words and make a sentence.

hanche	lèvres	pincer	boisson
anca	labbra	pizzicare	bevanda

Name

Draw a Picture

I Can...

- [ ] use a Capital Letter
  The cat is big.

- [ ] use spaces

- [ ] sound out words
  d-o-g = dog

- [ ] use a Period .

- [ ] Draw a picture

Name: _______________________ Date: _______________

Today is: [Monday] [Tuesday] [Wednesday] [Thursday] [Friday]

Name: _______________________ Date: _______________

Today is: Monday Tuesday Wednesday
Thursday Friday

Direction: Read the words and make a sentence.

en forme	**frappé**	**trousse**	**asseoir**
in forma	colpire	kit	sedersi

Name

Draw a Picture

I Can...

- [ ] use a Capital Letter
  The cat is big.

- [ ] use spaces

- [ ] sound out words
  d-o-g = dog

- [ ] use a Period .

- [ ] Draw a picture

Name: _______________________   Date: _______________

Today is: Monday   Tuesday   Wednesday   Thursday   Friday

Name: _________________________ Date: _________________

Today is: | Monday | Tuesday | Wednesday |
| Thursday | Friday |

Direction: Read the words and make a sentence.

| **blé** | **emploi** | **rob** | **pleurer** |
| mais | lavoro | rapinare | piangere |

Draw a Picture

Name: _______________   Date: _______________

Today is: Monday Tuesday Wednesday Thursday Friday

Name: ______________________ Date: ______________

Today is: Monday Tuesday Wednesday

Thursday Friday

Direction: Read the words and make a sentence.

chien
cane

porc
maiale

le jogging
jogging

bois
legna

Name

Draw a Picture

I Can...

- [ ] use a Capital Letter
  <u>T</u>he cat is big.

- [ ] use spaces

- [ ] sound out words
  d-o-g = dog

- [ ] use a Period .

- [ ] Draw a picture

Name: _________________________ Date: _____________

Today is: Monday Tuesday Wednesday Thursday Friday

Name: _______________________ Date: _______________

Today is: Monday Tuesday Wednesday Thursday Friday

Direction: Read the words and make a sentence.

punaise	étreinte	cruche	agresser
insetto	abbraccio	brocca	boccale

Name ______________________________

Draw a Picture

I Can...

- [ ] use a Capital Letter
  The cat is big.

- [ ] use spaces

- [ ] sound out words
  d-o-g = dog

- [ ] use a Period .

- [ ] Draw a picture

Name: _____________________ Date: _____________

Today is: Monday | Tuesday | Wednesday
Thursday | Friday

Name: _________________ Date: _______________

Today is: Monday   Tuesday   Wednesday   Thursday   Friday

Direction: Read the words and make a sentence.

lit	point	chaud	pot
letto	punto	caldo	pentola

Draw a Picture

I Can...

use a Capital Letter
The cat is big.

use spaces

sound out words
d-o-g = dog

use a Period .

Draw a
picture

Name: _______________________ Date: _______________________

Today is: Monday   Tuesday   Wednesday
           Thursday   Friday